The Movement Towards Christian Unity in the Nineteenth Century

Christopher Dawson

Edited by Rene Kollar, O.S.B.

Saint Vincent Archabbey Publications
Latrobe, Pennsylvania

Copyright © 2003 Julian Scott
Introduction Copyright © 2006 Saint Vincent
Saint Vincent Archabbey Publications
Published by arrangement with Mr. Julian Scott,
literary executor of the author.

All rights reserved. No part of this book may be reproduced or transmitted in any form or by any means, electronic or mechanical, including photocopying, recording or by any information storage and retrieval system without permission in writing from the Publisher.

Library of Congress Cataloging-in-Publication Data

Dawson, Christopher, 1889-1970.
    The movement towards Christian unity in the nineteenth century / Christopher Dawson ; edited by Rene Kollar.
       p. cm.
    "A Wimmer memorial lecture"—Cover.
    Includes bibliographical references.
    ISBN 0-9773909-0-X (pbk.)
      1. Catholic Church—England—History—19th century.
      2. Christian union—Catholic Church.
      3. England—Church history—19th century.
      I. Kollar, Rene. II. Title.

BX1493.D39 2006
280'.042094209034—dc22

2006049137

Printed in the United States of America
Archabbey Publications
300 Fraser Purchase Road
Latrobe, Pennsylvania 15650-2690
http://www.stvincentstore.com

Cover photo of Christopher Dawson courtesy of
The Department of Special Collections,
University of Saint Thomas, Saint Paul, Minnesota

Book design by Kimberley A. Opatka-Metzgar
Saint Vincent Archabbey Publications
Public Relations Assistant, Sarah Yaple
Saint Vincent Archabbey Archives Assistance provided by
Rev. Omer U. Kline, O.S.B., and Br. Matthias Martinez, O.S.B.

Contents

Introduction 5
Wimmer Memorial Lectures 9
Christopher Dawson 10
Lecture Invitation 11
The Wimmer Memorial Lecture 15
Illustrations 35
Correspondence 41

Introduction

Roman Catholicism and the place of Catholicism in public life could easily inflame passions and incite violence in Victorian England. Examples of religious prejudice frequently appeared in parliamentary debates, newspapers, works of fiction, and the oratory of itinerant speakers. Since the Henrician Reformation of the sixteenth century, Catholics were viewed as serious threats to the well-being of the body politic, and consequently a series of laws excluded them from political and public life and discriminated against them because of their beliefs. Following the French Revolution, however, some toleration was extended to English Roman Catholics. Catholic Emancipation (1829), which gave them the right to sit in Parliament, especially upset some Britons. Moreover, the large number of immigrant Irish Catholics and the Restoration of the Hierarchy in 1850 frightened many who believed that the Protestant character of their nation might be under siege. Christopher Dawson's 1960 Wimmer Lecture, "The Movement Towards Christian Unity in the Nineteenth Century," explores the rebirth of English Catholicism and how it sought to heal the religious divisions created by misunderstanding and centuries of intolerance.

Born in 1889, Christopher Dawson was educated at Trinity College,

Oxford, where he studied modern history, and while an undergraduate, he converted to Roman Catholicism.[1] Dawson graduated in 1911, and his reputation as a historian and writer grew. According to his entry in the *New Oxford Dictionary of National Biography,* Dawson "campaigned for an integrated study of Christian philosophy, history, literature, and art in the same way as *literae humaniores* had studied every aspect of classical culture. Only this, he believed, could overcome the schism between religion and culture in the West."[2] Dawson made his name as a scholar outside of traditional academic circles, but in 1958, at the age of sixty-nine, he and his wife, Valerie, traveled to Harvard University where he would occupy the Stillman Chair in the Divinity School until 1962.

Without any extensive experience in the lecture hall, this appointment presented challenges to Dawson, but "Harvard felt well satisfied by Christopher Dawson's presence there and it was generally thought that with his quiet but persuasive personality and his learning he was the right occupant for the first Stillman Chair."[3] Dawson presented lectures dealing with the relationship between Catholicism and western culture, the Reformation, and a series of lectures describing the movement toward Christian unity in the nineteenth century.[4] The latter formed the basis for his Saint Vincent College Wimmer Lecture. Dawson and his wife also spent much time traveling throughout America, a country which he admired, and accepted numerous invitations to lecture on Catholicism. Officials at Saint Vincent College recognized Dawson's importance as a spokesperson for Catholic values and the liberal arts, and invited him to speak at the Latrobe campus.

Archabbot Denis Strittmatter, OSB, the monastic superior at Saint Vincent Archabbey, and Fr. Quentin Schaut, OSB, the President of Saint Vincent College, began a correspondence with Dawson in May 1958 with the intention of asking him to give the Wimmer Lecture in December of that year.[5] These letters between Saint Vincent and Harvard, which appear in this book, not only reveal how valued Christopher Dawson had become as a lecturer in America, but also the hectic nature of his schedule and his failing health. Because of his new responsibilities at Harvard, Dawson declined this first invitation from Archabbot Denis. In early spring 1959, Saint Vincent asked him again, and this time Dawson accepted. December 6 was agreed upon as a tentative date for the lecture. During the summer and fall, Fr. Quentin frequently exchanged letters with Dawson concerning travel arrangements and possible topics, but on November 24 Professor Dawson's secretary informed Saint Vincent that he had been hospitalized and his visit had to be cancelled. By early March 1960, however, Dawson had regained his strength, and the Wimmer Lecture was rescheduled for April 7. On that date Christopher Dawson and his wife arrived at Saint Vincent to present his lecture, "The Movement Towards Christian Unity in the Nineteenth Century." The invitation reprinted in this publication is the announcement of Dawson's talk scheduled to take place in 1959.

One of the Saint Vincent Benedictines who attended this talk recalls Dawson's frail condition and his weak speaking voice, but this monk also remembers the favorable impression which the speaker's words had on the large audience. After some laudatory remarks about American Catholicism, Dawson discussed the rebirth of English Catholicism and the part played by John Henry Newman, Nicholas Wiseman, and Edward Manning in this spiritual and intellectual renaissance. Both Newman and Manning, he pointed out, had succeeded in breaking down the "cultural division which had so long separated Catholicism from the life of the nation." According to Dawson, schism is evil because it destroys God's plan for unity among people. Dawson ended his lecture with a plea for Christian unity: "And the tragedy is that schism could be removed if all Christians willed it, as for the most part they say they do—and they are usually sincere or not consciously insincere in saying so." Christopher Dawson was certainly optimistic as the Catholic Church prepared for the upcoming work of Vatican Council II, and had he lived longer, Dawson would have approved of the Council's decree on unity among Christians.

After Dawson returned to Harvard, Fr. Quentin began the process to have the Wimmer Lecture published. Dawson sent him some revisions, but this project was never completed. Because of his minor stroke in 1959, Dawson had delayed his lecture at Saint Vincent by several months. In 1962, he suffered another stroke, and consequently he made the decision to leave Harvard and to return to England. He and his wife departed from New York for England in July 1962. Christopher Dawson died on May 25, 1970, and his writings still continue to attract attention.

Christopher Dawson's 1960 Wimmer Lecture still has relevance today in a world split by discord, religious division, and schism within Christianity. Editorial changes to Dawson's typescript are few. I have included the appropriate reference citations and made some minor corrections in direct quotations. A special thanks to Mr. Julian Scott, Christopher Dawson's grandson and literary executor, for permission to publish this lecture. All works by Christopher Dawson Copyright © Julian Philip Scott, 2003.

—Rene Kollar, O.S.B.

Notes

[1] For a biography of Christopher Dawson, see Christina Scott, *A Historian and His World. A Life of Christopher Dawson 1889-1970* (London: Sheed & Ward, 1984). This book also contains a bibliography of Dawson's works. Scott was Christopher Dawson's daughter.

[2] *Oxford Dictionary of National Biography*, s.v. "Dawson, (Henry) Christopher (1889-1970),"

[3] C. Scott, *A Historian and His World*, 190.

[4] Ibid., 192.

[5] Materials relating to Christopher Dawson's Wimmer Lecture, including the correspondence between Dawson and Saint Vincent, are located in the Saint Vincent Archabbey Archives, Latrobe, Pa.

Wimmer Memorial Lectures

Kenneth J. Conant, "Benedictine Contributions to Church Architecture" (1947) *
Erwin Panofsky, "Gothic Architecture and Scholasticism" (1948)*
Gerald B. Phelan, "The Wisdom of Saint Anselm" (1949)*
Pitirim A. Sorokin, "The Crisis of Our Age Grows" (1950)
Jacques Maritain, "Man's Approach to God," (1951) *
William Foxwell Albright, "Towards a Theistic Humanism" (1952)*
Hugh S. Taylor, "The Catholic Intellectual in the Christian Economy" (1953)
Helen C. White, "Prayer and Poetry" (1954)*
E. A. Lowe, "The Finest Book in the World" (1955)
Stephan G. Kuttner, "Harmony from Dissonance: An Interpretation of Medieval Canon Law" (1956)*
Henri Maurice Peyre, "The Problem of Sincerity in Contemporary French Literature" (1957)
John Ching-Hsiung Wu, "Christian Influences in the Common Law" (1958)
Christopher Dawson, "The Movement Towards Christian Unity in the Nineteenth Century" (1960)
Ignatius T. Eschmann, "Moral Theology Today" (1960)
Paul Oskar Kristeller, "Renaissance Philosophy and Mediaeval Tradition" (1961) *
Gerhart Burian Ladner, "Ad Imaginem Dei: The Image of Man in Mediaeval Art" (1962) *
Frederick D. Rossini, "Some Reflections on Science and Thermodynamics" (1963)
Jean Alfred Ladriere, "Possibility and Task of a Philosophy of Nature" (1964)
John Tracy Ellis, "A Commitment to the Truth" (1965)*
Henry Margenau, "Scientific Indeterminism and Human Freedom" (1966)*
Gunnar Myrdal, "The Problem of Objectivity in Social Research" (1967) *
Howard Mumford Jones, "History and Relevance" (1968)*
Paul Weiss, "Theology and Verification" (1969)
Paul Goodman, "Silence, Speaking, and Language" (1970)*

* **Published.**

*Photo of Christopher Dawson courtesy of
The Department of Special Collections,
University of Saint Thomas, Saint Paul, Minnesota*

VERI IUSTIQUE SCIENTIA VINDEX

Wimmer Lecture
1959

the chancellor and directors

of

saint vincent college

cordially invite you to the

1959 wimmer lecture

to be delivered by

christoper henry dawson

on the subject

«the movement towards christian unity
in the nineteenth century»

the lecture will be delivered in the auditorium of sportsman's hall on sunday evening, december 6, at 8:15 o'clock

you are also invited to the reception
in the lounge of sportsman's hall after the lecture

CHRISTOPHER HENRY DAWSON

HUMANIST, SCHOLAR, LECTURER, TEACHER, EDITOR, AUTHOR. Born, Yorkshire, England, 1889. Winchester School; M.A., Trinity College, Oxford University; D.H.L., honoris causa, St. John's University (N.Y.), 1959.

Lecturer in the History of Culture, University College, Exeter, 1930–36; British Academy Annual Lecture on a Master Mind, 1934; Forwood Lecturer in the Philosophy of Religion, University of Liverpool, 1934; Editor, *The Dublin Review*, 1940–58; Fellow of the British Academy, 1943; Gifford Lecturer, University of Edinburgh, 1947, 1948–49; Charles Chauncey Stillman Guest Professor of Roman Catholic Theological Studies, Divinity School, Harvard University, 1958–.

Publications include: *The Age of the Gods* (1928), *Progress and Religion* (1929), *Christianity and the New Age* (1931), *The Making of Europe: An Introduction to the History of European Unity* (1932), *Enquiries into Religion and Culture* (1933), *The Spirit of the Oxford Movement* (1933), *Medieval Religion* (1934), *Religion and the Modern State* (1935), *Beyond Politics* (1939), *The Judgment of Nations* (1942), *Religion and Culture* (1948), *Religion and the Rise of Western Culture* (1950), *Understanding Europe* (1952), *The Dynamics of World History* (1957), and *The Movement of World Revolution* (1959).

The Movement Towards Christian Unity in the Nineteenth Century

Christopher Dawson

Wimmer Memorial Lecture
1960

"Surely the Second Volume was never intended, and is not adapted, to teach us our creed; however certain it is that we can prove our creed from it, when it has once been taught us, and in spite of individual producible exceptions to the general rule. From the very first, the rule has been, as a matter of fact, that the Church should teach the truth, and then should appeal to Scripture in vindication of its own teaching."

John Henry Cardinal Newman,
The Arians of the Fourth Century
(London: Longmans, Green and Co., 1919), 50.

The Wimmer Memorial Lecture

Of all the problems that engage the attention of the Catholic historian, the question of Christian unity is the most central and the most fundamental. The Church is one as Christ is one, and He Himself prayed on the last day before his Passion that this unity should be inseparably bound up with the unity of the divine nature and should be to the world the visible proof of the divine mission.

> "That all may be one, even as you, Father, in me, and I in You, that they also may be one in Us, that the world may believe that you have sent Me"
> (John 17:21).

Nevertheless, from the time of the apostles to the present day the Church has been engaged in an unceasing warfare to preserve and defend this divine gift, and again and again through the centuries she has had to suffer from schism and to see whole churches and nations torn away from the unity of the One Body.

What makes this experience more grievous is that in the majority of cases schism is the work of an active minority and that the passive majority are carried into schism without any deliberate intent and often without being conscious of what has been done by their rulers. But when a schism has once taken place, it becomes enlarged and fortified by the action of social and political forces until the religious division becomes a cultural one and the gulf becomes so wide that mutual understanding becomes impossible.

We have seen an outstanding example of this in our own Western history. The great breach of religious unity which caused the greater part of northern Europe to be torn away from the Church was followed by an age of strife in which religious and secular forces became inextricably mingled. The Catholic and Protestant peoples became divided from one another not only by theological controversy but by religious wars and national rivalries until they no longer shared a common spiritual or social experience. They became two different worlds, each with its own culture and its own social inheritance, as well as its own religious beliefs and its own standards of orthodoxy. The schismatic principle continued to operate, so that whatever religious unity the Protestant world originally possessed disappeared in a chaos of competing sectarianism.

Nor was the Catholic world immune, for in the seventeenth and eighteenth centuries, the spirit of schism was kept alive by Jansenism and Gallicanism until at last, with the French Revolution, the unity of the Church in France was destroyed by the Civil Constitution of the Clergy in 1790.

Never has the cause of Christian unity seemed more hopeless than at the end of the eighteenth century. The Church in France and Belgium was reduced to a persecuted remnant, and in Germany and Italy the same anti-Catholic forces seemed about to triumph. Rome itself was occupied by the armies of the Revolution and Pope Pius VI was carried into captivity to France, where he died a prisoner at Valence on August 28, 1799.

But though no one at the time could have realized it, this moment marks the turn of the tide of history—the end of three centuries of continually increasing schisms and divisions and the gradual beginning of a new movement towards unity. The nineteenth century was not an age of triumph for the Church—on the contrary she seemed defeated and rejected, and the papal encyclicals show how dark the prospect appeared to the Popes themselves. Nevertheless it was a time of new life and the beginning of a new age of Catholicism.

I have just described how the centuries of schism had divided the peoples from one another by frontiers that were both religious and cultural, so that in America, for example, the English-speaking Protestant North and the Spanish-speaking Catholic South formed two closed worlds, completely alien to one another in their ways of life and without even the possibility of religious contact or of spiritual understanding. This state of segregation had endured for centuries and there seemed little prospect of its ever changing. But at last in the nineteenth century Providence interfered and changed the whole situation by the action of impersonal historical forces. For in the course of the nineteenth century a series of political and economic changes produced a new movement of population in the Western world. Millions of European workers and peasants left their homes and came to seek a new life across the Atlantic.

The first great mass migration consisted of Irish Catholics, and they were directed by the force of circumstances to the cities of the Atlantic seaboard—to Boston and New York and Philadelphia—which were the centers of the American Protestant tradition. They came in thousands and in millions, and they were followed by other national groups—Germans and Italians, Poles and Czechs, the majority of whom were also Catholics. They established themselves in the cities, which they remade, for it was with the mass immigration that the modern urban development of America began.

For a long time they remained separate peoples since there was no intellectual contact and little social contact between Catholics and Protestants. Nevertheless, they shared a common citizenship and ultimately came to share a common culture, though of necessity it was a purely secular culture, since as yet there was no spiritual bridge between the two sections of the population. All the same, they had come together and formed one people—the modern American nation. And here for the first time since the Reformation the social segregation of Catholics and Protestants had been ended—not by their conscious acts, but by the decree of Providence, so that the two religious communities are living together in the same state and sharing the same culture.

This state of things was brought home to me very forcibly when I came to America for the first time, a year ago, to teach at Harvard. Here was a great stronghold of American Protestant culture with the tradition of three hundred years of learning and leadership, and all around one saw the growing mass of Catholic population with its churches and schools and colleges and religious orders, which has made Boston almost a Catholic city. This is a very striking phenomenon, and it makes one ask oneself what it all points to and what is going to come of it.

It is difficult for a Catholic not to see the hand of God in it. The creation of this great American Church out of nothing, in the midst of a society which seemed as far away from Catholicism as any society in Christendom, was not the result of human planning and design: it was God's work, not man's—as great a miracle as anything we read of in the history of the past. God has, in fact, intervened in history to undo the social consequences of the Reformation by ending that state of cultural segregation that kept Catholics and Protestants apart from one another by the differences of nationality and culture. He has, so to speak, forced them together and made them share the same social world and speak the same language and employ the same ways of thought and feeling (for that is what a common national culture means).

But have we done our part? Have we made the most of the opportunities that this new situation offers for the Catholic apostolate and for the cause of Christian unity? American Catholics may certainly congratulate themselves on what they have achieved during the last hundred years. They started with nothing—without material resources or intellectual resources or cultural traditions—for the traditions that they brought with them from the Old World were often an obstacle rather than an advantage under the new conditions that they had to meet. But in spite of all the disadvantages, at the price of much sacrifice and devotion and hard work, they came through and built that great fabric of Catholic institutions which is the foundation of modern American Catholicism. Thus they did the work that lay to their hands, and in doing so they built Catholicism into the life of modern America. That was the essential task of the Church in the nineteenth century and indeed up to the period of the World Wars; and until that had been done, nothing else was possible.

Though the creation of this new American Catholicism is the most impressive example of the new forces of creation and expansion that were at work in the Church in the nineteenth century, it does not stand alone. The same process was at work in England though on a smaller scale. There also the nineteenth century saw the rebirth of Catholicism and its re-entry into the national life after centuries of persecution and proscription. And the history of the English development is even more instructive than the American, since this movement was intensely aware of the problem of religious disunity and inspired by the hope of a return to Catholic unity.

The rise of American Catholicism was due to a vast movement of population which had nothing to do with individual choice or intellectual considerations. The rebirth of English Catholicism owed its distinctive character to a movement which originated within the Protestant world and reestablished contact with Catholicism by breaking down the blind wall of ignorance and prejudice which had separated England from the Catholic world for so many centuries. It had its beginning in the University of Oxford, the stronghold of Anglican tradition, among the fellows of the Oxford colleges and the clergy of the Church of England. Its intellectual background was purely English and owed little or nothing to the influence of the contemporary Catholic revival on the continent. None of its leaders except Edward Bouverie Pusey knew anything of German thought, though a little, a very little, was known about France. And the greatest mind among them—that of John Henry Newman—was the most narrowly insular of all in its background.

Consequently, their approach to Catholicism came not through contemporary continental culture, but almost exclusively through the Fathers and the earlier Anglican theologians. Their piety was intensely biblical as we can see from Newman's and Henry Edward Manning's sermons—but they accepted the doctrine of tradition which distinguished the old High Church Anglicans from the Evangelical Protestants, viz., that "the sacred text was never intended to teach doctrine, but only to prove it, and that, if we would learn doctrine, we must have recourse to the formularies of the Church . . . [and] only after learning from them the doctrines of Christianity, the inquirer must verify them by Scripture."[1] What the Oxford Movement did was to revive the study of positive theology in the Church of England: to go from the Anglican formularies to those of antiquity and to the teachings of the Fathers of the Church.

Thus the movement developed in an atmosphere of intensive historical study. And in the course of their patristic studies Newman and his friends were led to realize that Catholic antiquity was essentially Catholic and that the Anglican tradition, at least so far as the Reformers were concerned, was to a great extent Protestant, so that a return to Catholic antiquity might involve not only a reform of current Anglican practice, but also a breach with the formularies of the Anglican Church. And when Newman's *tour de force* in the interpretation of these formularies in a Catholic sense, the famous *Tract 90*, was disavowed by his own university and bishop in 1841, he was brought face to face with the necessity for a decision. Nevertheless, he found the decision exceedingly hard to make, and it took him four years of agonizing intellectual and moral examination to sever the links that bound him so closely to the Church of England and the University of Oxford.

It was the witness of history that finally convinced him. "To be deep in history," he wrote once, "is to cease to be a Protestant."[2] And in the same way, as he shows in the *Essay on Development,* the cumulative evidence of the Christian past led him on to a full acceptance of the Catholic present. There were but two paths—the way of faith and the way of unbelief, and as the latter led through the halfway house of Liberalism to atheism, the former led through the halfway house of Anglicanism to Catholicism. Thus his final destination was already implicitly present in the Evangelical faith which was his starting point. As he wrote at the very end of his life, ". . . those great and burning truths which I learned when a boy from Evangelical teaching, I have found impressed upon my heart with fresh and ever increasing force by the Holy Roman Church . . . That Church has added to the simple Evangelicalism of my first teachers, but it has obscured, diluted, enfeebled, nothing of it."[3]

No convert has ever made a more careful and conscientious

approach to Catholicism, testing every step, weighing every alternative and considering every objection. It is not surprising that his final decision was anticipated by some of the younger members of the movement, notably by W. G. Ward, the most brilliant of his disciples, who was a man of completely different temperament and training and who cut the Gordian knot of the Anglican position by the sharp edge of logic instead of unraveling it patiently by the slow process of historical inquiry. But the very fact that Newman had delayed his decision for years made it all the more effective when it finally came. The Oxford Movement had lost its intellectual leadership (Pusey also had been suspended in 1843 for two years), and its very survival seemed uncertain. The spirit of Oxford itself changed very abruptly, for the younger men who did not follow Newman into the Church followed the other path of which Newman spoke and reacted either to Liberalism like A. P. Stanley or to unbelief like Mark Pattison and J. A. Froude.

On the Catholic side the coming of the converts was received with mixed feeling. The earlier converts and their friends among the old Catholics, above all Dr. Nicholas Wiseman, greeted it enthusiastically as marking the beginning of the return of England to the Faith. But the majority of the old Catholics took a much less sympathetic attitude. The fact that the converts came from the very heart of the Establishment, from the ranks of the Anglican clergy who were their hereditary enemies did not predispose the Catholics to look on them with favor. Moreover Newman's philosophy and his whole mentality was strange to them. Their outlook was very insular and very conservative with no room for new ideas. Consequently, they tended to share the ordinary plain Englishman's view of the Oxford Movement as an inconsistent attempt to claim a Catholic character for a Protestant tradition. They could understand the position of a downright Protestant, but they were completely incapable of understanding the Anglo-Catholic *Via Media* of Newman and Pusey.

Typical of these old Catholics was the Vicar Apostolic of the London District, Bishop Thomas Griffiths, who wrote to Prince Hohenlohe of Munich in 1842 that "The leaders of this party seem to have no leaning to the Catholic Church itself, but wish to recover as much as they can of Catholic doctrine and practice without submission and union to the true Church."[4] And elsewhere he wrote, ". . . we occasionally find them [the schismatics] acknowledging some truths which they had formerly rejected as errors, and approaching in particular tenets nearer to the true Church which they had abandoned; but scarcely shall we find a body of schismatics returning with sincerity to the true Faith."[5]

But at Rome a very different view was taken and Pope Gregory XVI himself wrote to the London clergy rebuking their own bishop [Griffiths] in the most outspoken terms for his lack of understanding and appreciation of the work of the Puseites–Puseiti:

> "What is the reason why nearly every man of keen intelligence, and many too among the less gifted multitude acknowledge against their will that the Catholic Faith is moving not with slow steps in England, but is with amazing and irresistible advance returning again to its ancient home? In a word, what race at any time, where the Catholic religion has once been lost, has ever been able to show the most learned of those in schism in its richly endowed Universities, searching out all the arguments of antiquity, setting them forth without a thought of self-interest, publishing them in abundance for the general good as we may to-day see done by the Puseyites?"[6]

In taking this view the Pope was no doubt influenced by Dr. Wiseman who was the great advocate of the movement at Rome; and when Bishop Griffiths died less than two years later, Wiseman was immediately appointed as his successor and soon afterwards became a Cardinal and the head of the restored English hierarchy.

Wiseman was the son of an Irish merchant in Spain. He was born and brought up at Seville and educated in England at Ushaw College; but the greater part of his early life, from 1818 to 1840, was spent at Rome at the English College. Thus he had a threefold connection—with Ireland, with England, and with the continent—so that he was exceptionally fitted to unite the divergent elements in English Catholicism. It was peculiarly fortunate that he was chosen to be the head of the restored Catholic hierarchy in England at the beginning of the new era, for he was a man of European culture and wide sympathies and he was singularly free from the provincialism of the old English Catholics and the national prejudices of the Irish. He was the first to realize the importance of the Oxford Movement for the Church; and in 1841 he published a remarkable letter to the Earl of Shrewsbury, the leader of the Catholic laity, in which he looks forward to the speedy return of the Anglican Church to Catholic unity and urges the English Catholics to cooperate with the followers of the Oxford Movement to bring this about.

This was written before the great wave of conversions in 1845, and it is not surprising that after this occurred Wiseman was convinced that the conversion of England was at hand and that he saw the restoration of the English hierarchy in 1850 as the confirmation of his hopes. Unfortunately, he did not realize the strength of anti-Catholic feeling in England. His announcement of the establishment of the new hierarchy, and still more the triumphant tones in which his announcement was expressed, aroused the dormant bigotry of English Protestantism; and the country was suddenly swept by a violent wave of anti-Catholic feeling. It was at the same time that an even more violent storm of religious intolerance was sweeping the United States, so that in both countries the peaceful penetration of Catholicism into the Protestant world met with a serious setback which rendered friendly relations and mutual understanding difficult. Nevertheless it did nothing to weaken the movement of conversions, for it was in the midst of this anti-Catholic agitation that Henry Edward Manning joined the Church, as well as his friend Robert Wilberforce and many others.

Manning was to be the greatest influence on the Catholic revival in England after Newman, and it was unfortunate that their incompatibility of temperament caused them to appear as opponents rather than allies in their common cause. Newman had the retiring temperament of a scholar and a poet, combined with an intense sensitiveness which made him resent the slightest criticism or neglect. He was only happy in the intimate atmosphere of the Oratory and of his personal friendships. Manning was a man of iron will and self-control who subordinated his private life and his personal relations with others to the service of Catholicism and the cause of the Papacy. He was a statesman and a man of the world who moved wisely in Victorian society; he was a friend of many eminent Victorians and cultivated any public relations that could be of service to the cause he had at heart.

Yet this does not mean that he was the narrow-minded, hardhearted, ambitious prelate of Lytton Strachey's portrait. He was an extremely remarkable personality, a man of wide views and wide sympathies—wider even in many respects than those of Newman, though in a different direction. For instance, it was Manning, not Newman, who took part in the meetings of the Metaphysical Society, where so many leading Victorians of every shade of opinion—Catholic, Protestant and

Agnostic—gathered in friendly discussion. It was Manning rather than Newman who was most alive to the new social problems created by the industrial age and who took the lead in impressing on Catholics their responsibility for the conditions of the workers. And finally, in spite of his uncompromising dogmatic orthodoxy he became increasingly aware of the ecumenical problem and showed a very large-minded appreciation of the religious values and truths preserved by English Protestantism. His great complaint against the old Catholic tradition in England was that it had narrowed these sympathies and caused them to shrink from participation in public life and social action.

This double apostolate of Newman and Manning—one intellectual and addressed to the few, the other social and addressed to the nation—succeeded in breaking down the cultural division which had so long separated Catholicism from the life of the nation. Manning believed that the whole civil and political life of England was now open to Catholics, if they knew how to enter and how to conduct themselves.[7] Perhaps the most striking example of the changed situation was the conversion of Lord Ripon, one of the leaders of the Liberal party and a former Grandmaster of the English Freemasons who was to become the first and only Catholic Viceroy of India.

Such an occurrence shows that nothing is impossible, given the requisite leadership; but we must remember that even leaders like Newman and Manning are not enough. Their work was made possible by hundreds of individual conversions and each of these conversions meant the building of a new bridge by which it was possible to pass from schism to Catholic unity.

Now the two methods by which Catholicism came back into the English-speaking world—the American method of creating a Catholic mass community in the midst of a Protestant population, and the English method of creating individual points of contact with the Protestant world—are complementary to one another and in the twentieth century they are both becoming common to the two areas. American Catholicism is becoming more conscious than in the nineteenth century of the opportunities for an intellectual apostolate among non-Catholics, and English Catholicism is acquiring a wider basis in the masses owing to the growing Irish immigration and the steady growth of the Catholic population.

Nevertheless the present century has not yet seen any new movement as remarkable as was the planting of Catholicism in the West during the nineteenth century in America or as the conversion of the leaders of the Oxford Movement in England. This is certainly not due to any lack of concern for the cause of Christian unity. On the contrary, it has never been more in the minds of Catholics than today when we are on the eve of an Ecumenical Council [Vatican Council II] which will be especially dedicated to this problem.

In the English-speaking world the obstacles to the work of Christian unity are still very great and the old prejudices against the Catholic Church are very far from dead. But there are signs, as I said earlier, of a turn of the tide—men's minds are turning against the idea of schism; and throughout the Protestant world there is a widespread movement of return to the idea of Christian unity. In this country during the recent years there has been a very remarkable development of ecumenical discussion between Catholics and Protestants which finds its characteristic expression in the volumes of essays by representatives of the different religions—Catholics and Protestants or Catholics, Protestants, and Jews—which are now a characteristic type of American religious publication.

In a recent article in *The American Benedictine Review* Dom Kilian McDonnell has listed a whole series of such books together with other ecumenical literature, and it is evident that a serious effort is being made by Catholics and Protestants alike to understand the ground of their differences and to explain their religious position to one another in an irenical spirit. This meeting of minds is a new phenomenon in America. Throughout the 19th century there was a physical mingling of Catholics and Protestants with a certain amount of social intercourse, but no real contact on the intellectual and spiritual level. No doubt there are vast tracts of American life that are unaffected by this dialogue, not only on account of religious conservatism and intolerance, but much more because the ordinary American today has not the theological or even secular culture to make such discussions intelligible. Yet it seems that America is a very favorable field for the development of an experiment of this kind, for the vast expansion of higher education during the last twenty or thirty years is creating a new literate public and a new atmosphere in which ideas can be freely ventilated.

But it is still limited in two directions—first by the failure of American public education to prepare the mind for any kind of religious or theological culture and secondly by the failure of Catholic education to produce an adequate number of thinkers and writers who are able to speak to the outside world in a language that it can understand. This failure is only relative. We are producing writers and interpreters in increasing numbers, but there are not enough of them; and we have yet to find a spokesman who can speak to the American Protestant world of the twentieth century as Newman spoke to the English Protestant world a century ago. Such men are rare, it is true, and not every age can produce them. But at least we can ask that the highest intellectual capacities that we actually possess should be devoted to these tasks.

Our great misfortune at the present time, especially I think in this country and in Ireland (to which American Catholicism has owed so much) is not that the Catholic community fails to produce men of outstanding intellectual and literary ability, but that in the majority of cases these potential intellectual leaders have been lost to the Church and have used their talents in other fields. It is invidious to mention names, but I think it is a fact that the leading writers of Catholic origin are not Catholic writers. Nor do I ask why this is so. But I feel that the answer to this question must lie in the field of Catholic education.

But the ultimate problem is not a purely intellectual one: it is a question of spiritual leadership. The loss of Christian unity in the age of the Renaissance and the Reformation was due to a failure of spiritual leadership on the part of the Church and to the fact that the Reformers, in spite of their dogmatic errors, were the leaders of the age. Every turning point in history is an opportunity for leadership and every age has the leaders it deserves. If Catholics fail to grasp the need of the hour, then the leaders will be schismatics, and if the Christians fail, then the leadership will pass to the non-Christians and especially to the revolutionary leaders who understand how to unloose the forces of destruction. Such leaders may not be "great men" in the old sense of the words, as we see in the case of the men like Hitler who in our own time have changed the pattern of history. But in every case the leader is one who responds to the demands and opportunities of his age so that the final responsibility rests not with the leader himself but with the people who have nourished false hopes and worshipped false ideals until they have created a leader in their own image.

Now, the same principle holds good in the spiritual world and in matters of religion. Christendom has not recovered its unity because the will to unity has been weak and divided. If the will to unity were strong enough and pure enough, it would create the necessary organs of unity. Rainer Maria Rilke, who was not, I think, a practicing Catholic, but a man of Catholic traditions, once wrote that his generation had lost its faith because it had lost its sense of communion so that every man was absorbed in his own particular ideas and fears: "We are always spinning out one faculty of understanding that it may suffice us, instead of crying out to the iconostasis of our common misery, behind which the Inscrutable would have time to gather itself and put forth all its strength."[8]

If Christians possessed this urgent sense of common spiritual need, if they could concentrate their unrealized resources of prayer and faith on this central issue, they would find that the obstacles to Christian unity which now seem so insurmountable would disappear like the ice blocks in a river in spring. The time is ripe for a great change, but we still lack the common consciousness of our common spiritual need.

Nevertheless we all know as one of the great primary truths of the Christian faith that the Catholic Church has been created by God as the one universal, divine society which is common to all nations, whatever their differences of race and language and political citizenship—the common home of redeemed humanity in which alone man becomes free from that burden of inherited evil that has always frustrated man's natural efforts to create a better social order.

Schism is thus the worst of evils for it ruins God's own design for human unity by bringing war and dissension inside the walls of the City of God. And so long as schism and division between Christians exist, the Church's work for humanity is impeded and obstructed on the deepest spiritual level. If schism could be abolished, it is impossible to imagine how great the spiritual consequences might be. And the tragedy is that schism could be removed if all Christians willed it, as for the most part they say they do—and they are usually sincere or not consciously insincere in saying so. At least the fact that they say this and the existence of a will to unity among the separated Christians is a reason for hope and an encouragement to Catholics to play their part. If we do this, we cannot doubt that God will open new paths for the realization of His purposes as He did in the nineteenth century. God is at work in history renewing the face of the earth, and no one knows what the future—even the immediate future—has in store.

Notes

[1] John Henry Newman, *Apologia Pro Vita Sua* (London: Longmans, Green, and Co., 1897), 9. Newman is referring to a sermon on tradition preached by Dr. Edward Hawkins at St. Mary's, Oxford, which he heard while an undergraduate.

[2] John Henry Newman, *The Development of Christian Doctrine* (New York: Longmans, Green and Co., Inc., 1949), 7.

[3] Wilfrid Ward, *The Life of John Henry Cardinal Newman,* vol. 2 (Longmans, Green and Co., 1912), 527.

[4] Quoted in Bernard Ward, *The Sequel to Catholic Emancipation*, vol. 2 (London: Longmans, Green and Co., 1915), 96.

[5] Ibid., 101.

[6] Ibid., 102.

[7] For Manning's view on this subject, see "The Work and the Wants of the Catholic Church in England," in *Miscellanies* (New York: The Catholic Publication Society, 1877). This article originally appeared in the *Dublin Review*, July 1863.

[8] This quotation is from Rilke's *The Notebooks of Malte Laurids Brigge.* For another translation, see Egon Schwarz, ed., Rainer Maria Rilke. *Prose and Poetry* (New York: Continuum, 1984), 138.

Illustrations

Archabbot Denis Strittmatter, O.S.B.

Rev. Quentin Schaut, O.S.B.

Saint Vincent Campus, circa 1960

Kennedy Hall, circa 1960

Auditorium in Kennedy Hall, circa 1960
Photo Copyright © Michael Fedison, West Penn Power

Correspondence

May 15, 1958

Professor Christopher Dawson
c/o Sheed and Ward, Inc.
840 Broadway
New York 3, New York

Dear Professor Dawson:

During our centennial we established an annual lecture in honor of Archabbot Boniface Wimmer, the founder of this institution and of the Benedictine Order in America. The lecture is delivered on some convenient date near December 8th, the anniversary of Boniface Wimmer's death. I am writing to invite you to deliver the lecture this year.

In the choice of a topic the lecturer enjoys complete freedom. Though the work should be scholarly, it need not be highly technical, addressed only to other scholars. In due course the lecture is published in the form of a small book. Perhaps you have seen the one by Professor Erwin Panofsky, *Gothic Architecture and Scholasticism*, published in hard covers by us, and subsequently as a paperback in Meridian Books. A list of the lectures already given is enclosed.

The audience at the lecture is composed chiefly of the faculty and students of St. Vincent College and Seminary. The honorarium is two hundred dollars. If the suggested date would not fit into your schedule, please do not decline for that reason. I am sure we could agree on a suitable date. As for location, we are an overnight trip, with direct train service, from Boston; by plane a few hours.

We hope much that you will find it possible to accept this invitation, for we are well aware that you would make an outstanding contribution to what we believe to be a distinguished series of lectures. We are especially eager to welcome a Catholic scholar of your dimensions.

Sincerely yours,
(Rt. Rev.) Denis O. Strittmatter, O.S.B.
Archabbot

Hermitage
Budleigh Salterton,
Devonshire

20th May, 1958

Dear Archabbot,

Thank you for your letter of 15th May, and I am complimented by your kind invitation to deliver a lecture in honor of Archabbot Boniface Wimmer the founder of your institution.

As you will have heard, I have recently been appointed to a Professorship at Harvard University for a period of five years and I am afraid that, for this year anyway, I shall not be in a position to accept your invitation owing to the exigences of my new work. I much regret having to refuse your offer.

Yours sincerely,
Christopher Dawson

June 24, 1958

Professor Christopher Dawson
Hermitage Budleigh Salterton
Devonshire, England

Dear Professor Dawson:

An unduly long period has elapsed since I received your letter of May 20, a period during which we have been occupied by the heightened activity connected with the closing of the school year and then by our annual retreat which places limitation on activities.

I am indeed sorry to learn that you feel it unwise to accept our invitation to deliver the Wimmer Lecture here this year. To be sure, I fully appreciate the wisdom of your decision to decline invitations of this kind, at least during the first year of your tenure at Harvard. I hope, however, that you will keep our Wimmer Lecture in mind, for I am sure we shall wish to approach you again after you begin feeling at home in your new position and environment.

Take my best wishes for complete success in your work at Harvard. Everyone I know was more than happy to read of this appointment.

Sincerely yours,
(Rt. Rev.) Denis O. Strittmatter, O.S.B.
Archabbot

January 26, 1959

Professor Christopher Dawson
Harvard University
Cambridge, Massachusetts

Dear Professor Dawson,

Perhaps you will recall my writing to you last May to invite you to deliver our 1958 Wimmer Lecture. At the time you felt it unwise to commit yourself to anything of this kind during your first months at Harvard, to the atmosphere of which—if not to the unusual temperatures this year—you have no doubt become acclimated by this time.

I now repeat the invitation in the earnest hope that you will be able to accept it this year. A date somewhere near the feast of the Immaculate Conception is the usual time for the lecture, though there is nothing rigidly fixed about it. The subject is likewise entirely at the choice of the lecturer. Later the lecture is published in the form of a small but, we have often been told, rather attractive book. The lecture now carries an honorarium of two hundred and fifty dollars.

Again I am enclosing a list of the scholars who have honored us in this series. We should be more than happy to add your distinguished name to the list.

I know you will give this invitation your serious consideration, and I trust I may receive a favorable reply. Even apart from the lecture, I think you might enjoy a visit to this oldest Benedictine house in America. Meanwhile I send best wishes for your health and all other blessings.

Sincerely yours,
(Rt. Rev.) Denis O. Strittmatter, O.S.B.
Archabbot

HARVARD DIVINITY SCHOOL
45 Francis Avenue
Cambridge 38, Massachusetts

11A Traill Street
Cambridge, Massachusetts
February 3, 1959

Rt. Rev. Denis O. Strittmatter, O.S.B.
Archabbot
Saint Vincent Archabbey
Latrobe, Pennsylvania

Dear Archabbot Strittmatter,

Thank you for your letter of January 26. I am very interested in participating in your Wimmer Lecture series, and I am honored by your invitation. However, my decision depends upon the date of the proposed lecture. In our letter you mentioned that the lecture was usually held somewhere near the feast of the Immaculate Conception. I am puzzled as to whether this means the very near future or next winter (December, 1959).

My lectures here at Harvard make it difficult for me to leave during the academic term, which closes in May. So, if the lecture is scheduled for anytime in February, March, or April, I fear it would be impossible for me to come. However, I think something could be arranged for late spring or next fall or winter. Please advise me on this matter.

Yours sincerely,
Christopher Dawson

CD:mb

February 10, 1959

Professor Christopher Dawson
11A Traill Street
Cambridge, Massachusetts

Dear Professor Dawson:

We are delighted to know that you are in a position to accept our invitation to deliver the 1959 lecture. Your decision makes us very happy.

I note that the decision is somewhat tentative depending upon the date for the lecture. I am afraid my previous letter was not very clear on this point.

The lecture for this academic year has already been delivered. Yours would be on December 8, 1959, or some time near that date. Looking over the calendar, I find that Sunday evening, December 6, might be most suitable. It would enable you to get back to Cambridge by Monday afternoon, if necessary, since a midnight train from here will take you to New York by about 7:30 a.m. If neither December 6 nor December 8 is a good date for you, do not hesitate to suggest another. You might even wish to move into January. In that case, the date selected would have to fall between January 5 and January 26. Fridays and Saturdays would be ruled out.

I shall look forward to learning your preference in regard to a date. Meanwhile, let me say again that we are highly pleased to know that you will honor our Wimmer Lecture series by participating in it. Take my best wishes for your good health and success in your work at Harvard.

Sincerely yours,
Denis O. Strittmatter, O.S.B.
Archabbot

11A Traill Street
Cambridge, Massachusetts
KIrkland 7-6915

February 16, 1959

Denis O. Strittmatter, O.S.B.
Archabbot
Saint Vincent Archabbey
Latrobe, Pennsylvania

Dear Father Archabbot,

Many thanks for your letter of February 10. I shall be glad to lecture on the date you mentioned which is December 6, 1959, a Sunday evening. I will write you again later with regard to the subject.

Yours sincerely,
Christopher Dawson

CD:mb

Saint Vincent Archabbey
Latrobe, Pennsylvania
February 27, 1959

Professor Christopher Dawson
11A Traill Street
Cambridge, Massachusetts

Dear Professor Dawson:

It is a very great pleasure to acknowledge your letter of February 16, in which you accept the date, December 6, 1959, for our Wimmer Lecture.

We know that your appearance here will be the highlight of the academic year.

All good wishes.

Sincerely yours,
Denis O. Strittmatter, O.S.B.
Archabbot

October 28, 1959

Professor Christopher Dawson
11 A Traill Street
Cambridge, Massachusetts

Dear Professor Dawson:

    The date for the Wimmer Lecture, December 6, is no longer very far away, and so we are turning to preparations for it. One of the things that we do is print an invitation which we send to a limited number of people. For this purpose, we need the title of your lecture. If you can give me this title now, I shall be grateful.

    We had hoped you might be able to spend some time with us after the conclusion of your visit with Bishop Wright last summer, but the good Bishop informed us that you were going from Pittsburgh to Maine.

    I hope you and Mrs. Dawson are well. Every good wish.

                                      Sincerely yours,
                            (Rev.) Quentin L. Schaut, O.S.B.
                                              President

HARVARD DIVINITY SCHOOL
56 Francis Avenue
Cambridge 38, Massachusetts

November 6, 1959

Rev. Quentin L. Schaut, O.S.B.
St. Vincent College
Latrobe, Pennsylvania

Dear Father Schaut,

Thank you for your letter. I am much looking forward to my visit at St. Vincent College. I am wondering if my article on "The Movement Towards Christian Unity in the 19th Century" would be a good lecture.

Mrs. Dawson will by accompanying me on the visit. Our plans, at present, are to fly to Pennsylvania on Saturday, December 5, and to return to Cambridge on Monday, December 7.

Yours sincerely,
Christopher Dawson

CD:mb

November 9, 1959

Professor Christopher Dawson
56 Francis Avenue
Cambridge 38, Massachusetts

Dear Professor Dawson:

Many thanks for your letter of November 6, which contains the unexpected but very pleasant information that Mrs. Dawson will accompany you on your visit to Saint Vincent in December. We shall be more than happy to welcome both of you.

I am not quite certain of the implications of your statement, "I am wondering if my article on 'The Movement Towards Christian Unity in the Nineteenth Century' would be a good lecture." The topic certainly would be a most acceptable one, but I am a bit puzzled as to whether you are thinking in terms of something you have already published in the form in which you would give it here. As you may recall, in earlier correspondence about the Wimmer Lecture, it is our practice to publish the lecture as a small volume. Several of them should appear soon, but you may have come across our hard cover edition of the one by Professor Erwin Panofsky (*Gothic Architecture and Scholasticism*). If the title you offer is a new one, we shall be more than happy with it.

Best wishes.

Sincerely yours,
(Rev.) Quentin L. Schaut, O.S.B.
President

HARVARD DIVINITY SCHOOL
45 Francis Avenue
Cambridge 38, Massachusetts

November 13, 1959

Rev. Quentin L. Schaut, O.S.B.
Office of the President
Saint Vincent College
Latrobe, Pennsylvania

Dear Father Schaut,

Thank you for you letter of November 7th. I am sorry that I misled you in my last letter. The article to which I referred has never been published.

I also have another unpublished lecture on "Medieval Education and the Rise of Vernacular Culture" which might be good for the Wimmer Lecture. This article is more historical than the one I suggested earlier on "The Movement Towards Christian Unity in the 19th Century." Which do you think would be most suitable?

Looking forward to our meeting in December.

Yours sincerely,
Christopher Dawson

CD:mb

November 17, 1959

Professor Christopher Dawson
56 Francis Avenue
Cambridge, Massachusetts

Dear Professor Dawson:

I am sorry I misconceived the intent of your letter in which you offered us a title for the Wimmer Lecture.

Both the titles you suggest in your letter of November 13 are attractive, and they create the difficulty of making a choice. All in all, however, we feel that "The Movement Towards Christian Unity in the 19th Century" will be more suitable for this occasion, and so we shall settle for that.

We try to make something of a ceremony of the Wimmer Lecture, and so we ask the lecturer to appear in academic garb. If it would be too inconvenient for you to bring a complete academic outfit with you, we could supply you with a cap and gown, but we would not, of course, have the proper hood for you. We should have to depend upon you to provide the hood you would wish to wear. No doubt I shall be writing to you again. However, to prevent any confusion, let me say that we have engaged a room for you and Mrs. Dawson at Mountain View Hotel, which is just about two miles from the College. If you come by plane to Pittsburgh and let me know the time of your arrival, we shall pick you up there. If you come by train, we shall meet you in Latrobe.

We are confident that the lecture will be an important one, and we look forward with very great pleasure to having you and Mrs. Dawson as our guests.

Sincerely yours,
(Rev.) Quentin L. Schaut, O.S.B.
President

HARVARD DIVINITY SCHOOL
45 Francis Avenue
Cambridge 38, Massachusetts

November 24, 1959

Rev. Quentin L. Schaut, O.S.B.
Office of the President
Saint Vincent College
Latrobe, Pennsylvania

Dear Father Schaut,

Professor Dawson was taken ill this weekend and it is now necessary to cancel all his appointments for the next month. He will be in the hospital for at least two weeks and will have to be very quiet for two or three weeks following his release. He is extremely sorry that he will not be able to deliver the Wimmer Lecture at Saint Vincent College as planned and hopes that he has not caused you irreparable inconvenience.

Yours sincerely,
Marietta Bisson
Secretary to Professor Dawson

November 30, 1959

Professor Christopher Dawson
Harvard Divinity School
45 Francis Avenue
Cambridge 38, Massachusetts

Dear Professor Dawson:

The distressing news of your illness came to me via telephone while I was attending the annual meeting of the Middle States Association of Colleges and Secondary Schools (the accrediting association for this region). Needless to say, I was sorry to hear this report—on your own account much more than because of the Wimmer Lecture.

We have sent out notices to the effect that the Lecture has been postponed, assuming that you would be willing to deliver the lecture later during the school year, after you will have fully recovered. I hope this assumption has your approval. The date can be determined later.

Along with our best wishes go our prayers for your speedy recovery.

Very sincerely yours,
Quentin L. Schaut, O.S.B.

HARVARD DIVINITY SCHOOL
45 Francis Avenue
Cambridge 38, Massachusetts

56 Francis Avenue
Cambridge, Massachusetts
December 4, 1959

Rev. Quentin L. Schaut, O.S.B.
Office of the President
Saint Vincent College
Latrobe, Pennsylvania

Dear Father Schaut,

Thank you so much for your letter and good wishes. I feel that I am recovering steadily and hope to be on my feet again for the holidays. I would like very much to deliver the Wimmer Lecture at a later date in the year. At present it is impossible for me to tell you when this would be but the doctors say that in a few weeks time they will know better how much work I shall be able to take up so I shall write you again after I confer with the doctors on this matter.

Yours sincerely,
Christopher Dawson

CD:mb

December 10, 1959

Professor Christopher Dawson
56 Francis Avenue
Cambridge, Massachusetts

Dear Professor Dawson:

It is most satisfying to know that you are steadily recovering your health and that you expect to be up and around for the holidays. I hope and pray your progress will continue apace.

I am very glad, too, with your assurance that this attack has not diverted your interest from the Wimmer Lecture. There is nothing to impel us to be hasty about selecting another date for it. When your doctors and you feel that the time is ripe, we shall be happy to agree with you on a convenient date.

Sincerely yours,
(Rev.) Quentin L. Schaut, O.S.B.
President

February 12, 1960

Professor Christopher Dawson
56 Francis Avenue
Cambridge 38, Massachusetts

Dear Professor Dawson:

We have been doing some further thinking about the Wimmer Lecture, nursing the hope that your health has improved steadily and markedly from the time it became necessary to cancel the December date.

I wonder whether it would be possible for you to think in terms of a definite date at this time. A number of Sunday evenings would be available: February 28, March 6, 13, 27, and April 3. There would also be possible dates during the week.

I hope I may hear that you are again quite well and ready to think about a visit to Saint Vincent.

Every good wish.

Sincerely yours,
(Rev.) Quentin L. Schaut, O.S.B.
President

HARVARD DIVINITY SCHOOL
45 Francis Avenue
Cambridge 38, Massachusetts

56 Francis Avenue
Cambridge, Massachusetts
February 19, 1960

Rev. Quentin L. Schaut, O.S.B.
President
Saint Vincent College
Latrobe, Pennsylvania

Dear Father Schaut,

Thank you for your letter of February 12th. I am very sorry to say that I have considered all the dates that you mention in your letter and find that none of them are possible times for me. But after the 3rd of April we have a recess here — from Monday April 4th, through the following weekend, April 8th, 9th, 10th — and I could come at any time during this week. Would any day during that week be good for you?

Yours sincerely,
Christopher Dawson

CD: mb

February 23, 1960

Professor Christopher Dawson
56 Francis Avenue
Cambridge 8, Massachusetts

Dear Professor Dawson:

Your letter of February 19 was a most welcome visitor. The time you suggest for the lecture, during the free period beginning the week of April 4, is quite satisfactory to us. The date that would be most convenient for us is Thursday, April 7.

The lecture, as you know, will be held at 8:15 in the evening. It has been our custom to ask the lecturer to appear in academic garb. We could lighten your luggage to the extent of supplying you with a cap and gown here, but we would not have on hand an appropriate academic hood.

It will be very fine indeed to have you on our campus. The title of the lecture, I take it, will remain the same, namely, "The Movement Towards Christian Unity in the Nineteenth Century."

All good wishes.

Sincerely yours,
(Rev.) Quentin L. Schaut, O.S.B.
President

March 8, 1960

Professor Christopher Dawson
56 Francis Avenue
Cambridge 8, Massachusetts

Dear Professor Dawson:

If the new date for the Wimmer Lecture, Thursday, April 7, 1960, is satisfactory to you, I should be grateful to have a word of confirmation. The Lecture was advertised in December as "The Movement Towards Christian Unity in the Nineteenth Century," and I assume that this remains the topic.

Western Pennsylvania is just beginning to emerge from a massive accumulation of snow, but I am confident that we can promise you good weather for April.

Every best wish.

Sincerely yours,
(Rev.) Quentin L. Schaut, O.S.B.
President

HARVARD DIVINITY SCHOOL
45 Francis Avenue
Cambridge 38, Massachusetts

56 Francis Avenue
Cambridge, Massachusetts
March 11, 1960

Rev. Quentin L. Schaut, O.S.B.
President
Saint Vincent College
Latrobe, Pennsylvania

Dear Father Schaut,

Thank you for your letter of March 8th. The new date for the Wimmer Lecture, April 7, is quite satisfactory to me. I am much looking forward to our visit at Saint Vincent College, and hope that my health will hold up until then. I still intend to give the lecture on "The Movement Towards Christian Unity in the Nineteenth Century."

Yours sincerely,
Christopher Dawson

CD:mb

March 15, 1960

Professor Christopher Dawson
56 Francis Avenue
Cambridge, Massachusetts

Dear Professor Dawson:

Many thanks for your quick confirmation of the date for the Wimmer Lecture. We shall now be able to inform our friends that it will take place on April 7 and that the subject will be the one you offered for December.

I assume that Mrs. Dawson will accompany you, and so we shall make reservations for your stay.

I, too, fondly hope that your health will continue to be good, and I shall offer a prayer to that end.

Sincerely,
(Rev.) Quentin L. Schaut, O.S.B.
President

HARVARD DIVINITY SCHOOL
45 Francis Avenue
Cambridge 38, Massachusetts

March 31, 1960

Rev. Quentin L. Schaut, O.S.B.
St. Vincent College
Latrobe, Pennsylvania

Dear Father Schaut,

Professor Dawson's doctor advises him not to travel and lecture on the same day, so if it is agreeable with you, Professor and Mrs. Dawson would prefer to travel to Latrobe on Wednesday, April 6th and spend Wednesday (and Thursday) night at Latrobe.

According to present plans, they will arrive in Pittsburgh on TWA Flight 469 at 2:50 P.M. on Wednesday, April 6th. They plan to return to Cambridge on Friday, leaving Pittsburgh at 1:00 P.M.

The Dawson's [sic] are very much looking forward to their visit to Latrobe.

With best wishes for a successful meeting,

Yours sincerely,
Marietta Bisson
Secretary to Professor Dawson